Art History Tarot for Past Lives

By: Red Orchid Publishing

Introduction

I have been reading tarot professionally for five years and own an established business as a spiritual consultant. As well as developing a thorough understanding of the cards, I am also a medium. I am the type of reader who invites Spirit to play a significant role in the tarot reading process. What you hold in your hands is the deck I wished existed: a tarot deck especially designed for reading past lives.

As I read past lives for my clients, the tarot often revealed interesting information that pertained to the querent's current life: phobias, fears, blockages, painful relationships, etc. Tarot was especially revealing and helpful for healing current life problems as read through a past life lens. However, I often had to abruptly leave the tarot and rely solely on mediumship to orient the past life in place and time. Typically, when reading for clients, I either use tarot for life questions, or mediumship to connect to deceased loved ones. The switch mid-reading was jarring and especially challenging. What if, I asked myself, we designated certain cards for countries and periods of time? Then I could allow the cards to flow through the session as they would in any other tarot reading.

Using art history as tarot images enriched the quality of this deck. Not only is the reading of your previous life a journey into the past, but the art itself arises from periods of time that have come and gone, perhaps providing another level of insight into who you may have been, where you left your mark, and what you may have done. I chose images from the public domain that provoked an emotional response when I gazed upon it, (as all excellent tarot images do) and I relied very heavily on the souls from the past and their beautiful art to bring this new system to you. So here I give a gregarious thank you to the talented artists who have gone before us and left their work to help us better understand ourselves. On more than one occasion, I felt a special connection to the artist as I selected their work, and felt the power of collaboration sustaining my efforts.

I feel a need to acknowledge that this deck is not as inclusive as it would ideally be. Much of art history is Eurocentric. Efforts were made to find artists and subject matter from diverse cultures, but as I was limited to royalty-free public domain images for this project, the deck does not include the range of history I would deem ideal. Please rely heavily on any diversity arising from the cards to find your truth.

Additionally, I would like to address the topic of gender. Although I firmly believe that we can transition between the two genders throughout lifetimes, for the purpose of reading past lives with this deck, it is important that gender identity remain fixed. Your mother was a woman, your brother was a man, etc. This is simply because you need a point of reference to ruminate effectively on the cards. Most needed messages that arise from your readings have nothing to do with gender and so simplifying this process will help keep the focus where it should be. Simply use whatever gender you or the person you are asking about identifies with in this life to draw connections.

There exists a unique and loving gathering of spirits willing and eager to assist you with this deck as you connect to the past, the divine, and your sacred path. May your journey into the past fortify your future.

Blessings Always,

Melanny Eva Henson

How to Read a Past Life with Tarot

It's important to remember that whatever information is arising from your past life is somehow relevant to your current path. There are many struggles reflected in the cards that are unpleasant: murder, starvation, drowning, premature death, etc. This angle is not intended to heighten the drama of your reading, but to point out past life struggles that are affecting you *now*. Spirit is attempting to deliver insight *for your current life*, so there is no reason to allow the fates of the past to upset you presently. If you starved in a past life, you might have an unreasonable relationship with food in this one. If you suffered poverty, you might be driving your current spouse crazy with how tight you are with money. The suffering of the past reveals the psychology of the present. My biggest piece of advice is to trust and allow what's true to come to you. Not every reading will punch you in the gut. Some readings are more revealing than others. Trust your instincts as you delve into this journey.

The Past Life Spread

There is no wrong way to use this deck, so feel free to use your own intuition to develop systems for using the cards and to design effective spreads. The following spread and description is intended as a starting point for the deck. I would also encourage you to pull two or three more cards on any of the cards in this spread if you are feeling particularly stuck in the interpretation.

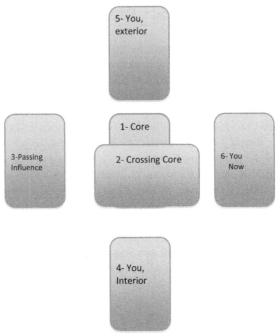

1- Core (Where/When)
2- Crossing Core (Where/When)
3- Passing Influence (What you still carry from this past life)
4- You, interior qualities
5- You, how others saw you
6- How this life is manifesting now

General Rules for Place and Time Cards

You may end up with more than one place or time card. Here are some general rules for reading such a spread:

1. The core and crossing core cards are your time and place cards. If a time or place card appears in either of these positions, they signify your concrete place and time. These positions are the "trump" for place and time. Core card trumps Crossing Core card.

2. If place and time appear in the surrounding cards, but not in the core and crossing core positions, they are read in this order, from most concrete to least concrete:

   A: **You Interior.** This position is traditionally "beneath the surface of the issue" and is most likely to signify concrete place and time if the core and crossing core do not.

   B: **Passing Influence.** Since this is traditionally the "past position" if place and/or time cards only lie here, they can be read as such.

   C: **You Exterior.** This is typically the "above the issue" or "vision" position, so should only be read as place/time if it is the only position that holds a place or time card.

   D: **You Now.** Since this is the traditional "future" position, it is least likely to denote place and/or time for a past life. Although this could possibly be place and time, they likely are not and should be read as place and/or time only if you feel a strong intuitive pull to do so.

3. When you have more than one place and time card, use the system above to identify the concrete place and time. With the additional card(s) read the core energy and alternate

interpretation of that card as explained in the book description.

4. The art itself can give additional clues about place and time. Check the country/artist information in the book and refer to the date on the card for time.

0-YOU

Traditional Card: The Fool

Root Energy: Fresh Start, naïve optimism, starting at the beginning

In a Past Life:

The You card in the deck is the one card that is used vastly different for a past life reading than it is for tarot. Whenever the You card appears, it refers to your direct spirit, the transition between lives, and the pure love that emanates from your spiritual essence.

If you pull the You card, the interpretation should be read in relation to you. All surrounding cards have more of a direct connection to you than they would otherwise, and all actions pertain to you: the loss card is your own loss, the drowning card is your own drowning, etc.

The You card carries The Fool energy in that it reflects the young optimism your spirit holds in each new incarnation, before the weights of life and past life problems come to the surface.

Place: Italy

Time: Renaissance

ABOUT THE ART

Filippino Lippi was living in Rome when he painted "Archangel Gabriel in the Annunciation." He was born and died in Florence, Italy and painted during the Florentine Renaissance. He was the illegitimate son of painter Fra Filippo Lippi and Lucrezia Buti, an Italian nun. Lippi studied under his father. Most of his work reflected biblical themes.

I- AFRICA

Traditional Card: The Magician

Root Energy: Resourcefulness,
manipulation,
manifestation

In a Past Life:

This card is rooted in the African
continent. Your past life is perhaps
rooted within Africa.

Alternative interpretation: If the card is
not read as a place card, it could denote the
use of occult magic, mystery,
resourcefulness, and the amazing ability to
produce what you want. Your ability to
produce results could be skills developed
from a previous life. This card could also
indicate a manipulative person.

Place: **Africa** (*Association between the
magician and the magic of deep
Africa*)

Time: 17th century

ABOUT THE ART

Although the artist is
unknown, this piece is
thought to represent the
role of Kizlar Agha, a
chief leader under the
Sultan of the Ottoman
Empire, eventually
ranking third in the
hierarchy by the 18th
century. The role was
filled by a black eunuch.
At its height, the
Ottoman Empire (1299-
1922) spanned an area
from Hungary in the
north to Yemen in the
south, and from Algeria
in the west to Iraq in the
east.

II- BEFORE CHRIST

Traditional Card: The High Priestess

Root Energy: Female magick, passive
and wise observation,
female authority,
psychic abilities

In a Past Life:

This card refers to the period before
Christ, primarily during earth-centered
religious practice.

Alternative interpretation: If the card is
not read as a time card, it could denote
psychic abilities in a past life; a woman who
is wise and slow to act as she observes the
events unfolding before her; or worshipping
the goddess. Your past likely includes a
nature-centered life without the restrictions
of formal religion.

Place: Belgium

Time: Before Christ;
all of AD - 0 BC;
alternatively, early 17th century

ABOUT THE ART

Jacob Jordaens resided in
Belgium his entire life
and did not study in Italy
like many of his
contemporaries. His
work is primarily biblical
and Greek myths,
including this painting,
"Offering to Ceres,
Goddess of the Harvest"
from 1619. Early
Goddess worship
involved sympathetic
magic to produce crops,
so the use of this art as
representing the High
Priestess, (the roots of
female divinity) is quite
apt.

III- MOTHER

Traditional Card: The Empress

Root Energy: Mother, nurturer, creativity, feminine power

In a Past Life:

Someone in this life was your mother in a past life. In the presence of the You card, it means you were the mother/parent in a past life to someone very close to you now.

Alternative interpretation: If a parent interpretation doesn't resonate, this card could also denote the life of an artist with abundant creativity. It's possible the creative talents you possess now were developed and refined in a past life, making certain artistic talents easier to grasp.

Place: America (Pennsylvania) or France

Time: Early 20ᵗʰ Century

ABOUT THE ART

Mary Cassatt built a reputation over her mother-and-child portraits such as this piece, "Mother and Child with a Rose Scarf" from 1905. She refused to be labeled a "women's artist" seeing her work and her subject of equal interest to both genders. She was fiercely independent and insatiably ambitious. She never married, and she painted devotedly until losing her eyesight in 1914. Born American, she spent her childhood and adolescence traveling abroad, and moved permanently to France in 1866 at age 22.

IV- FATHER

Traditional Card: Emperor

<u>Root Energy:</u> Father, worldly power, politics, powerful man

In a Past Life:

Someone in this life was your father in a past life. In the presence of the You card, it means you were the father/parent in a past life to someone very close to you now.

Alternative interpretation: This is the card of worldly power, so the reign of world leaders during a lifetime had a significant impact on that life. Example: a German living during Nazi Germany would have much of their life shaped by Hitler's leadership. It's also possible that the quest for worldly power is a desire you have brought from a past life experience.

Place: Amsterdam

Time: Early 17th century

ABOUT THE ART

Govert Flinck was the son of a silk mercer, but his passion for drawing and etching brought him into the lives of like-minded painters. This piece, "Isaac Blessing Jacob" from 1638, is his first subject painting. The similarities of his style to Rembrandt is notable, and indeed he studied the master's art extensively in order to better develop his own talent. He was born in Kleve and died in Amsterdam.

V- RELIGION

Traditional Card: Hierophant

<u>Root Energy</u>: Organized religion, institutions, clergy, schools

In a Past Life:

Religion played a heavy role in a past life and left an indelible print upon your soul. It's possible the religion you gravitated toward first in this life carried a significant connection to your past, leaving you feeling very much at home within that religious group. You might discover that leaving religion behind you carries some guilt because of social obligation and your deep roots within that system connecting you to the past.

Alternative interpretation: This card could also indicate formal education, or a person who is associated with a formal clergy. Official recognition is the trump energy of this card.

Place: Italy

Time: Early 16th century

ABOUT THE ART

This depiction of Isaiah from The Sistine Chape by Michelangelo di Lodovico Buonarroti Simoni adorns the ceili of the Vatican. It is a small piece of a 500-meter composition bas on narratives from the Old and New Testamen Michelangelo toiled aw in the chapel from 150 1512. From the church was painted upon, to th biblical prophet depict in the image, to Michelangelo's unsurpassed reputatio this art piece exudes th spiritual authority and established institution grounding reflected in Hierophant energy.

VI- LOVERS

Traditional Card: The Lovers

Root Energy: True love, critical choice, sexual union

In a Past Life:

Typically, this card appears when a lover you have/had in this life is a repeat occurrence from a past life. This card will usually appear when the romance was short lived in this life, leaving a gaping hole in your heart as you attempt to sort out what went wrong. This card is assuring you the deep pain you are feeling is a reservoir of emotions carried from a past life. You are not crazy or pathetic. Spirit and your guides are validating the deep pain you feel.

Alternative interpretation: If romance doesn't make sense for your spread/question, this card can indicate a critical choice—one that changed your path forever. It's very possible that this choice either haunts you now in the form of anxiety, or is a critical impasse that you will repeat in this life. In short, a do-over. Read surrounding cards to determine which interpretation makes the most sense.

Place: France

Time: 18th Century

ABOUT THE ART

Louis Jean Francois Lagrenee was both born and died in Paris. Aside from a few years in Rome studying art, he spent his entire life there, and built a career from an art scholarship he acquired in his youth. This piece, "Mars and Venus, Allegory of Peace" from 1770 is intended to represent gods, though the couple's candid pose and facial expressions are undeniably human. Mars has laid his sword and shield to rest, and one dove offers sustenance to another. In this image, the sexual passion that is often so volatile has been entirely accepted and integrated.

VII- AMERICA

Traditional Card: The Chariot

Root Energy: Drive/determination, transportation, going separate ways, making a choice

In a Past Life:

A past life was lived on the American continent, including possibly South America or Canada.

Alternative interpretation: This card could also indicate transportation or industry, or a parting of the ways between two souls. It's possible the fiery drive you have in this life is a continuation of the determination you once had in a previous life.

Place: **America** alternatively, **Spain** (*Association of the drive to migrate west from the chariot and the American continent*).

Time: Early 16th century

ABOUT THE ART

"The Virgin of the Navigators" by Spanish painter Alejo Fernande was painted sometime between 1531 and 153 During this period, extensive travel to the New World accelerated Concurrently, within Catholicism Mary bega to emerge as a primary figure of motherhood, (and all things good) a Marian art, as well as Mary's spiritual authority, grew to be more commonplace. Here, she protects the faithful and watches ov explorers as they sail t America.

VIII- STRENGTH

Traditional Card: Strength

<u>Root Energy</u>: Recovery from a
deep wound,
connection to animals

In a Past Life:

You are carrying a deep wound that
spans lifetimes. It is highly likely that
this hurt has occurred in more than
one past life. Whatever your deepest
wound may be now, your guides are
letting you know you have experienced
this pain more than once, so the hurt is
more intense for you than it might be
for others.

Alternative interpretation: This card
could also indicate a past life connection
to one of the animals in your home, or
an affinity for animal communication
that you developed in a past life.

Place: Italy (Genoa)

Time: Mid-17th Century

ABOUT THE ART

This Italian painting,
"The Death of Sampson"
from 1650 probably
came from the Geonese
School, though the artist
is unknown. The
Republic of Genoa was an
independent state from
1005-1797 on the
northwestern Italian
coast. Here, the biblical
Sampson uses his
supernatural strength to
destroy his enemies,
while also bringing about
his own death. The
Strength card, however,
reflects healing, so the
death in this image
becomes symbolic of the
new life that emerges
when the lions have been
tamed, and the threats to
our happiness have been
neutralized.

IX- ASIA

Traditional Card: The Hermit

Root Energy: Wise counselor, meditation, withdrawal from society, teacher

In a Past Life:

A past life was lived within the Asian continent.

Alternative interpretation: This card could also refer to a past life as a teacher, monk, or spiritual counselor. If you are drawn to meditation, Buddhism, or sabbaticals, it could be a manifestation from a previous life path. As a spiritual teacher in this life, you developed these skills in a previous life.

Place: **Asia** alternatively, **Kishangarh, Rajasthan, India** (*Association of meditation prolific in religion on the Asian continent*)

Time: 18ᵗʰ Century

ABOUT THE ART

The artist of this 1750 painting, "Akbar and Tansen visit Swami-Haridas in Vrindavan" is unknown. A popular narrative explains that Swami-Haridas was a saint and also a great musician. The emperor Akbar enjoyed his music so much, he wanted the saint to join his court. But Swami-Haridas was not a man of the world and declined. With his attendant Tansen, Akbar was compelled to secretly visit Swami-Haridas in his homeland of Vrindavan to hear him play privately for the Lord. It's a beautiful allegory about the spiritual benefit of abandoning the world and ego in pursuit of the soul.

X- FATE

Traditional Card: Wheel of Fortune

Root Energy: Fateful occurrence,
big change, shift in luck

In a Past Life:

When the Fate card lands in your spread, there's a message about your destiny. You probably just went through or are about to go through a huge shift or transition in your life. This change was predetermined before you entered this life as something you desired to learn and grow from. An event in a past life has inspired the desire to experience this change. For example, if you are in an abusive relationship, it could be that you desired to re-experience the abuse, but this time end the relationship, or perhaps you worked it out with your abuser to give him/her another chance to get it right, particularly if the person is a parent. Whether the relationship must end in this life or not, a karmic contract exists between you.

Alternative interpretation: Expect a change of luck in the near future as the good karma from the past catches up with you.

Place: Britain; alternatively, Iran

Time: 19th Century; alternatively, 1st century

ABOUT THE ART

"The Roll of Fate" by Walter Crane from 1882, is based off a translation of a poem by Omar Khayyám, a Persian mathematician, astronomer and poet born in northeastern Iran and who lived from 1048-1131. The art depicts an angel attempting to stop Time from unrolling the scroll of human destiny.

Walter Crane was born in Britain and built a career as a children's book illustrator. He grew to be considered one of the best children's book creators of his generation.

XI- JUSTICE

Traditional Card: Justice

Root Energy: Karmic balance, fairness

In a Past Life:

In a past life reading, the justice card does not carry the same "legal system/paperwork" connotation that it does for a traditional tarot spread. For a past life, justice means finally getting what you truly deserve and reaping benefits in this life that are owed to you from a past life. You might seem to be extraordinarily fortunate or lucky in this life, but it is your good thoughts and actions from the past creating balance with your life now.

Alternative interpretation: This card could be a warning to watch your negative thoughts and actions. Keep your negativity in check because you will eventually reap what you sow if you can't make peace in your heart. If you feel your life has been unlucky, draw upon your inner strength and take heart—good karma begins now and you have within you the power to shift the balance in your favor by focusing on love, generosity and gratitude.

Place: Germany; alternatively, Amsterdam

Time: 17th Century

ABOUT THE ART

Jürgen Ovens, recognized as a German painter, was living in Amsterdam when he painted "Justice" in 1662. A student of Rembrandt, he had just finished a piece by Govert Flinck (creator of the art on the "Father" card) who passed away before its completion. Interestingly, he owned three paintings by Jordaens, (creator of the art depicted in the "Before Christ" card).

The women in this piece represent Prudence, Justice and Peace. Justice reigns in the center, holding the sword of truth and the scales of justice. Does Peace want attention or is she intervening on someone's behalf?

XII- PREMATURE DEATH

Traditional Card: The Hanged Man

Root Energy: Suspension, a long wait

In a Past Life:

This is the card for unfinished business. A goal you had in a previous life remained unmet when an untimely death interrupted your work. Part of your mission in this life is to complete the goal you had set for yourself. When you reach this goal, your joy will be full and climactic because the wait and hard work spans lifetimes.

Alternative interpretation: You could have a spiritual block right now that is making it seem near impossible for you to move forward. This blockage is not limited to this life, but is rooted in a past life and fears carried from that life. If you have been recently asking yourself, *What is wrong with me?* this is probably the correct interpretation for this card.

Place: Berlin, Germany

Time: 19th Century

ABOUT THE ART

Hermann Anton Stilke, creator of "Joan of Arc's Death at the Stake" from 1843 was a German painter who studied at the Berlin Academy. His wife née Peipers was also a talented watercolor painter.

This art is part of a three-image triptych about Joan of Arc's life, currently on display at the Hermitage State Museum, in St. Petersburg, Russia.

XIII- DEATH

Traditional Card: Death

<u>Root Energy</u>: the end of a situation,
dramatic and wholistic change

In a Past Life:

The Death card could directly mean your death in an indicated life. It can just as likely mean that a dramatic change in your life now was spurred by an event in a past life. For example, you may have had a happy previous life in a pagan community. If organized religion has left you feeling unfulfilled in this life, you may make a dramatic shift at some point and leave that lifestyle behind. The Death card means the death of everything, so it indicates major changes in philosophy or lifestyle, a dramatic re-imagining that results in complete change. If you aren't experiencing a major transition currently, it likely indicates your literal death and that particular death's impact on your psyche now.

Alternative interpretation: The recent death of a loved one has you feeling down, but the past lives shared with this person keep your love and connection in-tact. This can be a loving message of comfort from the Holy Spirit during a period of grief.

Place: Paris, France

Time: 19th Century

ABOUT THE ART

The creator of this 1851 painting, "Angel of the Death" was Horace Vernet, son of famous painter Carle Vernet and grandson of famous painter Claude-Joseph Vernet.

Vernet was known for painting several leaders in France such as Napoleon III and he left his trademark by painting more reallistic poses rather than dramatic formalities often seen in Classicism.

The man in the painting prays for his companion's life as the angel of death lifts her towards heaven. Her peaceful expression reminds us that we need not fear change.

XIV- KARMIC LESSON

Traditional Card: Temperance

Root Energy: Balance, peace, self-control

In a Past Life:

The Karmic Lesson card indicates a lesson you have yet to grasp, one you have struggled with for more than one lifetime. It could be a simple weakness that creates imbalance, such as substance abuse, budgeting, or sex addiction. The pain you seek to bury reaches back into previous lives and is not manageable from only considering your current life and circumstances. Dig deep, pay attention to dreams, and sort through possible narratives to find the connection.

Alternative interpretation: The karmic lesson arising in this card could be someone else's, particularly if you are asking about someone else, or if you are at the mercy of someone else's temperance struggle at this time. Know that their pain is far-reaching.

Place: United States (Ohio)

Time: 19ᵗʰ Century

ABOUT THE ART

"The Temperance Lecture" by Edward Edmondson Jr. from 1861 depicts a self-indulgent father bowing his head in shame while his child cries. Temperance refers to the ability to self-regulate wisely to bring balance and peace to our lives.

Edward Edmonson Jr. was an American artist who worked primarily from Dayton, Ohio and was known for still life portraits.

XV- SLAVERY

Traditional Card: The Devil

Root Energy: Unhealthy attachment;
bondage

In a Past Life:

The Slavery card indicates a life framed by
slavery, most likely as the enslaved, but
possibly as the slave owner when in the
presence of the You card or the Greed
card.

If you were enslaved, you must work to
overcome a slave mentality: don't accept
meager wages or sell yourself short. Work on
eliminating fear of your boss or losing your
job. Control is an illusion, and the lack of
power in a past life can have lasting effects on
this one.

If you are the slave owner, you must work to
see the inherent value in all people. You are
likely a boss in this life and must work to pay
a fair wage and not profit off of the poor
circumstances of others.

Alternative interpretation: The slavery card
can indicate a slave mentality toward a
person, place or thing rather than centering
around employment.

Place: France
Time: 19ᵗʰ Century

ABOUT THE ART

"A Roman Slave Market"
by Jean-Léon Gérôme is
one of six slave market
scenes painted by the
artist, primarily for the
purpose of painting the
female form. This focus
somewhat blurred the
lines between slavery
and prostitution.

Gérôme lived and
studied primarily in
France. His work was
acknowledged, but he
often fell short of first-
class recognition or
securing the interest of
the public with his work.

Gérôme died in his
private studio in 1904.
He was found lying in
front of a Rembrandt
painting and one of his
own paintings, "Truth
Coming Out of Her Well."

XVI- PLAGUE

Traditional Card: The Tower

Root Energy: Dramatic and sweeping change; unforeseen destruction; removal of barriers; eliminating evil

In a Past Life:

The Plague card indicates a past life where a sweeping plague marked your life. In the presence of the Death or Illness card, you died from this plague. Look at geography and time clues to research the plague in history you were likely part of. This past life experience can manifest as germaphobia or hypochondria. Acute fears of losing loved ones unexpectedly could also occur in this life.

Alternative interpretation: Tower energy can also simply mean unexpected loss or destruction, possibly in this life, marked by an event from the past.

Place: Belgium or France

Time: 16th Century

ABOUT THE ART

Josse Lieferinxe, the creator of "Saint Sebastian Interceding for the Plague Stricken" from 1497-99, was simply known as the "Master of Saint Sebastian" until he was later identified in the 20th century. He was primarily known for an eight-scene retable depicting Saint Sebastian and Saint Roch, both saints considered protectors against the plague. Though born in Belgium, his adult life and art work centered in northern France.

XVII- EUROPE

Traditional Card: The Star

Root Energy: Hope; guiding inner light; soul's path

In a Past Life:

A past life was lived within the European continent.

Alternative interpretation: This card can also indicate a beam of hope, reassuring you that the current path you are on is in line with your soul's desire. A reading with this card present puts the focus on your current desires and offers you the reassurance that those desires are within reach.

Place: **Europe**; alternatively, **Germany** (Association of the guiding star and the migration to/from Europe)

Time: 16ᵗʰ Century

ABOUT THE ART

This image is likely a tailored reproduction of a piece by Heinrich Bünting, a German artist/pastor who composed ten creatively drawn maps for *Itinerarium sacrae scripturae, (1581)* his ambitious rewrite of the Bible as a travel book. In this image, Spain rests in Her crown, Germany at Her breast, and Italy as Her right arm.

XVIII- SOUTH AMERICA

Traditional Card: The Moon

Root Energy: Psychic insight; hidden truths; mystery; secrets

In a Past Life:

A past life was lived within the South American continent.

Alternative interpretation: This card indicates powerful psychic energy and insight, possibly carried from a past life. This card can also indicate an unknown and/or unseen element at play. The truth remains elusive for you, making it difficult for you to work through barriers because the cause of the issue is unclear. The power of the moon will eventually draw these truths to light for you.

Place: **South America** (Association of deep esoteric roots in South America and the mystery of the moon card)

Time: 1800 BC to 350 AD (Mayan history)

ABOUT THE ART

This Mayan art was found in Bonampak, Chiapas, Mexico, Fresco. War was a common theme in Mayan art. Tribal flags, costumes and clothing are drawn in great detail in this war image.

XIX- AUSTRALIA

Traditional Card: The Sun

Root Energy: Joy; children

In a Past Life:

A past life was lived within the Australian continent.

Alternative interpretation: This card is a lucky card of joy and fulfillment. It can also indicate the birth of a child, meaning a new child is about to enter this life with whom you share a powerful and sustaining connection. You will feel an immediate affinity for the child when you first see him/her, as a life together was once shared in a past lifetime.

Place: **Australia** (Association of Australian continent with the bright sun)

Time: 19th Century

ABOUT THE ART

Charles Hill, the creator of this 1836 painting, "The Proclamation of South Australia" was born in England and moved to Australia based on the advice that the weather would be good for his health. He found work as an art teacher, was a key participant in forming the South Australian Society of Arts, and became the first headmaster of the South Australian School of Design formed in 1861.

XX- THE MIDDLE EAST

Traditional Card: Judgment

<u>Root Energy</u>: Reckoning; new awareness; gaining clarity

In a Past Life:

A past life was lived within the Middle East.

ABOUT THE ART

Alternative interpretation: This card will appear when you are about to uncover a profound insight and gain much needed clarity about your life. Just as the political reckoning gestates and continues today in the middle east, so shall your life juggle a consistent internal conflict until a personal victory is won. After lifetimes of struggle, you are about to conquer the mental roadblocks that have held you back from realizing your full potential.

Place: **The Middle East**; alternatively, **Scotland** (Association of final judgment with the Middle East)

Time: 19th Century

David Roberts, creator of "Sphinx of Giza" from 1838, was primarily a Scottish landscape artist when a friend convinced him to paint full time. He then traveled to the Holy Land for several years. The subject matter was fashionable but nearly obsolete by other artists at that time, and he stayed very busy with commissions. He was working on painting in St. Paul's Cathedral in London when he died unexpectedly.

XXI- MIGRATION

Traditional Card: The World

Root Energy: Accomplishment;
      having it all; expansion

In a Past Life:

This card likely indicates the migration
from Europe to America, though other
migrations are possible as well.
Struggles from migrations from a
previous life could make it personally
difficult to travel over water or fly over
the ocean.

Alternative interpretation: This card is a
very positive card for attainment and
accomplishment. Gaining material success
you've longed for in the past is more
possible in this life than ever before.

Place: Belgium

Time: 17ᵗʰ Century

ABOUT THE ART

Andries van Eertvelt,
creator of "The Santa
Maria at Anchor" from
1628 is considered the
first Flemish marine
painter. Born in Belgium,
he spent a few years
studying painting in Italy
after his first wife's
untimely death. He then
returned to Belgium
where he began marine
life portraits. He is
believed to have taught
and mentored several
famous marine painters
such as Gaspar van Eyck,
Matthieu van
Plattenberg, Hendrik van
Minderhout,
Bonaventura Peeters,
and of Sebastian Castro.

TURKEY

Traditional Card: Ace of Cups

Root Energy: Potential for great love

In a Past Life:

At least a significant part of a past life was lived within Turkey. You may have Turkish ancestors.

Alternative interpretation: The Ace of Cups denotes a strong potential for unconditional love. Any relationships denoted in the spread have a far-reaching history of love within them. You should feel an unusual amount of acceptance from this person.

Place: **Turkey:** established October 29, 1923 (Scorpio/Water Sign/ Cup)

Time: 16ᵗʰ Century

ABOUT THE ART

This art by Geza Feher from 1931, depicts the 1521 Capture of Nándorfehérvár (Belgrade). The Christian Hungarians were able to defend an invasion from the Ottomans. The heroism displayed in this battle continues in reflective rhetoric today. Comparisons have been drawn between the Ottomans and modern-day Islam.

SPOUSE

Traditional Card: Two of Cups

Root Energy: Union

In a Past Life:

The relationship that appears in the spread is also connected to a spousal relationship at some point. If no other relationship cards are present, this card means the current spouse you have now was also your spouse in a past life. If you are not in a committed relationship now, your future spouse was also your past spouse.

Alternative interpretation: If romance or a spousal relationship doesn't resonate, this card can simply mean a long- term relationship between two parties that is mutually beneficial, such as a good career fit. A key job placement is rooted in past life connections.

Place: Spain

Time: Early 19ᵗʰ Century

ABOUT THE ART

José Gutiérrez de la Vega y Bocanegra painted "A Wedding in 1830" while his career as an artist was still budding in Europe. Born in Spain, he spent most of his life in Madrid and eventually gained favor with the queen for his work. The participants in this wedding are unknown.

FRIENDSHIP

Traditional Card: Three of Cups

Root Energy: Socialization; friendship

In a Past Life:

There's a friendship you are in now that is a continuation from a past life. This friendship should be one that deals in extremes at this time: either you are so close they are like family, or your relationship is very strained right now. Happy friendships are reunions from friends who were separated unwillingly in a past life. Sour friendships are an attempt to resolve karma.

Alternative interpretation: This card may simply be indicating a friendship or social function to orient the message of the spread, rather than illuminate the dynamics of the relationship.

Place: Poland

Time: 18th - 19th Century

ABOUT THE ART

Jozef Peszka was a Polish painter and art professor, known primarily for watercolor paintings. He painted mostly wealthy family portraits, and some landscapes as well as mythology paintings such as the Three Muses displayed here from 1800.

APATHY

Traditional Card: Four of Cups

Root Energy: Refusal,
discontentment, apathy

In a Past Life:

This card usually reflects the tendency to be unsatisfied, even when things are going right. In a past life reading, it often reflects something left undone that we wanted to accomplish in this life. It's also possible that the desires of your heart have past the due date on when they would have been achievable. Listlessness and a general lack of enthusiasm can spur from this past life disappointment.

Alternative interpretation: This card could also point to someone's refusal of you. It's possible someone left you high and dry without much explanation or justification. Such events are often rooted in a past life, at times directly related to the relationship you had with the person, and at other times stems strictly from an issue the person is working on individually.

Place: France

Time: Mid-18ᵗʰ Century

ABOUT THE ART

Jean-Baptise Greuze, painter of "Indolence" from 1756, was born in Tournus France. His father was vehemently against him becoming a painter, but a Lyonnese artist named Grandon convinced him to allow Greuze to become his pupil. He would grow to become a remarkable artist, with several of his paintings landing in the Louvre. His personality and style were known for "pleasures of disorder" as depicted here. He managed money poorly and died broke in the Louvre. Constance Mayer, a young female painter whom Greuze mentored, threw herself on his coffin at his funeral

LOSS

Traditional Card: Five of Cups

Root Energy: Acute disappointment;
hanging on to loss

In a Past Life:

A major loss from a past life is
haunting you in the present. Typically,
the type of pain the Loss card brings
comes from losing a treasured
relationship, a home, a life savings, or
access to food. What once
was is now gone. Sometimes this loss is
felt when we worked hard for something,
but never really attained it and was left
wanting in the end. Fears of losing again
can cause you to behave irrationally.

Alternative interpretation: The Loss card
could also be indicating a disappointment
you are struggling with in your current
life. The message here is that your
tendency to hang on is something you are
striving to work through and overcome in
this lifetime.

Place: England

Time: Early 20ᵗʰ Century

ABOUT THE ART

George Clausen was a
talented British
watercolor and oil artist
who worked as a
professor of painting at
the Royal Academy of
Arts in London. He was
an official war artist
during World War I. His
daughter's fiancé was
killed during that war,
which became the
subject of this 1916
painting, "Youth
Mourning."

KARMIC CONNECTION

Traditional Card: Six of Cups

Root Energy: Nostalgia, childhood, the past, good memories, karma, children

In a Past Life:

A relationship featured in this spread indicates a strong karmic connection: someone you are working through certain spiritual goals with in this lifetime. You share happy memories with this person, and this connection is likely to be an overall positive one. The strong spiritual connection you have to your children or an expected child is also indicated here.

Alternative interpretation: The six of cups might be pointing you to a past event in this lifetime that is connected to a previous lifetime. This would be a very intense event and likely the first thing that comes to mind. This card is traditionally the card of childhood, so something from your childhood or adolescence could be indicated here.

Place: United States

Time: Late 19th Century – Early 20th

ABOUT THE ART

Francis Davis Millet was born in Massachusetts in 1848. As a boy he worked as a drummer and as a surgical assistant to his father during the Civil War. He attributed his frequent use of blood red in his paintings to his experience working with his father. He graduated from Harvard with a Master of Arts degree and spent the first half of the 1870s living and painting in Rome. He died on the Titanic in 1912 and was last seen alive helping women and children into passenger boats.

POISON

Traditional Card: Seven of Cups

Root Energy: Illusion; fantasy;
Options; drink

In a Past Life:

It is possible that you suffered
from poison as the cause of death
in a previous life. If so, you're
likely to read the labels of most of
what you consume even if you're
not watching calories. It can also simply
mean misusing a substance that was at the
time believed to have health benefits but
was to your detriment, such as bleeding
with leeches, or developing scurvy.

Alternative interpretation: This card also
carries messages of illusion or fantasy,
struggling to stay grounded and indulging
in fantasy as a means to escape your
problems. It can also simply mean having
several options to choose from.

Place: Netherlands

Time: 17ᵗʰ to 18ᵗʰ Century

ABOUT THE ART

This Rembrandt painting
dated 1634 was
incorrectly identified for
centuries as Artemisia,
the Greek naval
strategist and
commander of Caria . She
consumed her dead
husband/brother's ashes
daily by miing them in a
drink. It was later
concluded that this
painting is a depiction of
Judith, who dined at the
banquet of Holofernes.
She discreetly beheaded
him, dispersing the
Assyrian army and
saving Israel. Whomever
Rembrandt meant to
paint, a lingering
question of what lies in
the cup overtakes the
narrative of this painting,
as an old woman watches
anonymously from the
shadows.

ABANDONMENT

Traditional Card: Eight of Cups

Root Energy: Walking away

In a Past Life:

The abandonment card indicates being abandoned in a past life. You may struggle with irrational fears of someone leaving you, or you may feel highly anxious about your children maturing and leaving home. If the You card is present, you are the one who abandoned someone else. You are likely positioned to assuage someone else's anxiety for being left as a means of balancing this karma.

Alternative interpretation: The root of the eight of cups means you have invested much of your time, energy and resources into something, but now have decided you must walk away from it. Although this transition is healthy, it's usually painful, whether you are the one leaving or being left. It can point to something you are walking away from right now, and the reasons why are rooted in past life experiences.

Place: Switzerland

Time: 18th Century

ABOUT THE ART

Maria Anna Angelika Kauffmann was a Swiss born painter who had a prolific career in London and Rome. Her father was poor, but a skilled muralist and painter. She moved to Rome with her father after her mother's death. She was one of two female founders of the Royal Academy in London in 1768.

The myth of Ariadne depicted in this 1774 painting is that Ariadne fell in love with Theseus and helped him escape certain death. In return he agreed to marry her but some versions of the story claim when they arrived on the island of Naxos, he proclaimed he didn't love her and faithlessly abandoned her.

CONGO

Traditional Card: Nine of Cups

Root Energy: Wish fulfillment

In a Past Life:

At least a significant part of a past life was lived within the Congo. You may have ancestors from this area.

Alternative interpretation: The traditional meaning of this card is having a dear wish granted. It's possible positive karma is due now, or that a wish left unfinished in a past life is being granted to you now.

Place: **Congo:** Established June 30, 1960 (Cancer/Water Sign/Cups)

Time: 15ᵗʰ Century

ABOUT THE ART

Albert Eckhout, born in the Netherlands, was one of the first artists to depict the New World on his journeys to Brazil. This painting, "African Warrior with Sword" from 1641 was during the same era as Ganga Zumba, the runaway slave leader originally from the Congo who organized a slave settlement in Brazil. This painting has often been associated with his legacy.

TWIN FLAMES

Traditional Card: Ten of Cups

Root Energy: Emotional completion

In a Past Life:

Everyone has a twin flame, though not everyone interacts with their twin flame in every lifetime. Sometimes, one twin remains in the spirit world to guide the other. Twin flames are dichotomous, one often assuming more feminine traits while the other assumes more masculine. They are traditionally portrayed in art as a heterosexual couple, but can very easily be a homosexual couple with similar polarities in place. These relationships tend to be turning points for the soul, usually short lived and volatile when ill-timed. Although exciting to experience, they rarely result in marriage as one twin is likely to either be frightened by the connection, or consider themselves superior in some way to the other, lacking the humility to embrace the full benefits of a twin flame connection.

Alternative interpretation: Traditionally, this card simply means complete emotional commitment and is a good omen for happiness.

Place: Germany (Munich)

Time: Late 19th Century

ABOUT THE ART

Bruno Piglhein, born in Germany, was the first president of The Munich Secession, a group of artists who were tired of the conservative control The Munich Art Association had over their work. Pieces by the artists in the Secession were considered more progressive, as evidenced by this noteworthy painting, "Pair of Lovers at the Spring" from 1890.

DAUGHTER

Traditional Card: Page of Cups

Root Energy: an offer

In a Past Life:

This card either refers to a daughter you have now, or a daughter you had in a past life, (and sometimes these are the same person!) With the You card, this means a role reversal where you were the daughter, and your daughter/child now was your mother.

Alternative interpretation: Traditionally, this card indicates the beginning stages of love: a crush, or the buddings of an emotional relationship. The ignited spark you are feeling at this time indicates a past life connection to the one you are forming desires towards. This card can often help identify what the spread is about because it indicates the one you have stomach butterflies over.

Place: Ireland

Time: 19ᵗʰ Century

ABOUT THE ART

Irish painter Augustus Nicholas Burke began his painting career at the Royal Academy in London. His paintings are quite rare because most of his studio was destroyed in a fire at the Abbey Street buildings of the RHA in 1916. This painting, Connemara Girl, from 1865, is from his homeland Connemara, a cultural region off the coast of Ireland.

HERO

Traditional Card: Knight of Cups

Root Energy: A loving gesture

In a Past Life:

You have committed acts of heroism in a past life. This can often indicate martyrdom. If so, you are likely to be spiritual and keep many spiritual items in your home. It can also indicate acts of bravery against oppressive systems of power, moments when you put yourself at risk to help others. The sacrifice has generated good karma for you.

Alternative interpretation: The knight of cups often means a forthcoming apology or a proposal of some kind. An offer is usually on the table. Expect good karma to arrive soon.

Place: Russia; alternatively Ukraine

Time: Early 19th Century; 10th Century

ABOUT THE ART

Russian painter Andrey Ivanov was abandoned by his parents and raised in a Moscow orphanage. He developed his talents and grew to become a Professor at the Imperial Academy of Arts.

The topic of this painting, "Young Hero from Kiev" from 1810, tells the story of a brave boy during the Siege of Kiev in 968. Knowing the enemy's language, he ventured through enemy camps to deliver a message to a general for the Queen of Kiev. His heroism allowed her to defeat the siege upon Kiev by the Pechenegs.

LOVING WOMAN

Traditional Card: Queen of Cups

Root Energy: Emotional woman, loving woman

In a Past Life:

The card of the Loving Woman denotes someone sensitive and kind. You will identify her by her loving nature, which began development in a past life. This card can also indicate a woman with generous amounts of love to give, often without an adequate outlet. She will choose heart over head in most cases.

Alternative interpretation: The negative side of the Queen of Cups is that she can be too emotional. Emotional problems are a higher risk with a cup person. This may be the case if the card is reversed.

Place: Switzerland and/or France

Time: Early 20th Century

ABOUT THE ART

Painter Gabriel Émile Edouard Nicolet was born in France and painted primarily in Switzerland. He is mainly known for female portraiture. This nurse from 1915 in "Portrait of a Nurse from the Red Cross" is most likely reflective of World War I.

BENEVOLENT MAN

Traditional Card: King of Cups

Root Energy: Emotional man;
Loving man

In a Past Life:

The Benevolent Man, above any other quality, has a good heart. He connects emotionally with people easily and is often a trusted confidant for others. Due to his great people skills, he often takes roles in clergy, counseling or social work.

Alternative interpretation: Like the Queen of Cups, the King of Cups is at higher risk for emotional issues and problems than the other suits. Sometimes he can be an emotional burden if he hasn't connected to his inner self yet. When reversed, he can reflect emotional problems like major depression or bipolar disorder.

Place: Greece and/or Spain and/or France

Time: 17ᵗʰ Century

ABOUT THE ART

Δομήνικος Θεοτοκόπουλος, most commonly known as El Greco (the Greek) was a painter, sculptor and architect of the Spanish Renaissance. His dramatic and expressionistic style wasn't as appreciated in his time as it is today.

Many historians concur that St. Louis IX, King of France, was perhaps the kindest king in history. He fed the poor at his own table, washed their feet, and worked on reforming homes after war raids.

KOREA

Traditional Card: Ace of Wands

Root Energy: Action; drive

In a Past Life:

At least a significant part of a past life was lived within Korea. You may have Korean ancestors.

Alternative interpretation: The traditional interpretation of this card is the drive to pursue something desired. When this card appears, your heart's desire is within reach and the universe is telling you to take action towards your dreams. This is very much a "go for it!" card, and the ideas you are contemplating now are connected to your past as well as your future.

Place: **Korea:** established 57 BC; North and South Korea split August 17, 1948 (Leo /Fire Sign/Wands)

Time: Middle Ages

ABOUT THE ART

Water-moon Avalokiteshvara is a buddhist bodhisattva who was worshipped for her ability to protect people from calamity and disease, and offering protection to travelers. This iconographic art style was prolific during the Goryeo period, (918-1392) though this particular painting (artist unknown) is dated around the first half of the 14th century.

CHINA

Traditional Card: Two of Wands

Root Energy: Planning; deciding

In a Past Life:

At least a significant part of a past life was lived within China. You may have Chinese ancestors.

Alternative interpretation: The traditional interpretation of this card is the planning stage before action is being taken. For a past life, it means the life path change you are ruminating on at this time is important to this life's goals.

Place: **China:** Established January 1, 1912 (Sagitarrius/Fire/Wands)

Time: Early 19th Century

ABOUT THE ART

Utagawa Kuniyoshi, born in 1798, was the son of a silk-dyer and helped his father design cloth patterns. He showed genius talent and was given an apprenticeship at Utagawa Toyokuni's studio. He struggled as a young adult to draw commissions, but a chance in counter with a less talented peer caused him to double his efforts, and he landed his first gig painting illustrations for the fictional story *Water Margin*. Chitasei Go Yo was an outlaw band's chief strategist and was nicknamed "Knowledgeable Star."

HIGH MIDDLE AGES

Traditional Card: Three of Wands

Root Energy: Action; drive; return on investment

In a Past Life:

You lived a past life in the High Middle Ages. This was a time of the Crusades and wars based on religion. Christians fought to push Muslims out. This Christianization led to the end of the Viking raids. This is the period when France and Germany were established.

Alternative interpretation: The three of wands is about acting toward something you want with the promise that the investment made will be worth it. Expect a karmic return.

Place: Germany

Time: High Middle Ages 1000-1250 AD

ABOUT THE ART

German painter Karl Friedrich Lessing studied art at the Berlin Academy. He was eventually appointed director of the gallery at Karlsruhe, and continued painting there until his death. This painting from 1835, "The Return of the Crusader," also known as, "The Last Crusader" depicts the end of the High Middle Ages when the Crusades were finally brought to an end.

LATE MIDDLE AGES

Traditional Card: Four of Wands

Root Energy: Stability; home;
structure; wedding

In a Past Life:

You lived a past life in the Late Middle
Ages. A series of plagues and famines
occurred during this period, including
the Black Death. France and England
experienced peasant uprisings, and this
was the period of The Hundred Years'
War. Despite all this strife, philosophy
and art still blossomed somewhat
during this period.

Alternative interpretation: The
traditional interpretation of this card is
about stability, such as the four posts of a
building. It often precedes happy, secure
times and can sometimes suggest a
wedding in the near future. When applied
to a past life, it would suggest a life lived
with general stability. Combined with the
chaos of the Late Middle Ages, this card
would mean exceptionally good luck
despite difficult times.

Place: Germany

Time: Late Middle Ages 1250-1400 AD

ABOUT THE ART

The Limbourg brothers
were three Dutch
miniature painters. They
had one very rich client,
The Duke of Barry, a
bibliophile who had
them illustrate *Tres
Riches Heures du Duc de
Barry* (The Very Rich
Hours of the Duke of
Barry). The Limbourg
brothers died (most
likely of the plague)
before they could finish
the project, but an
anonymous painter
began Its completion in
the 1440s.

CONFLICT

Traditional Card: Five of Wands

Root Energy: Competition; conflict of interests

In a Past Life:

This card could indicate major historical conflicts such as war, but could also simply reflect the conflict within a relationship, most likely a conflict that you are experiencing now. This conflict is likely rooted in a past life. The Hindu Gods observing the war in this card's image symbolize the universal presence that sees and knows all, including the injustices you have fought. When this card is present, peace is illusive, though not always violent. It can sometimes simply reflect a conflict of interests.

Alternative interpretation: This card could also mean competition. Is there someone in your life that you could clearly identify as your greatest competitor? If the answer is yes, this rivalry was likely established in a previous lifetime.

Place: India

Time: 16th Century

ABOUT THE ART

According to the Indian epic *The Mahabharata*, Arjuna was immaculately conceived by the god Indra. In this scene, he is coaxed by the god Krishna to lead a battle against his cousins the Kauravas, though he was at first hesitant to fight. The five gods watching from the heavens are most likely the five gods who immaculately conceived of Arjuna and his four brothers.

16TH CENTURY

Traditional Card: Six of Wands

Root Energy: Victory

In a Past Life:

You lived a past life in the 16th Century. This was a period of discovery, particularly of the American continent. This was a high- profile time for European explorers. However, for the indigenous people, it would spearhead the age of oppression that would continue for centuries.

Alternative interpretation: The six of wands usually reflects a victory won for the querent. Although in the image chosen here, a heavy reminder looms that many victories involve another's loss. Your life path may be pointing you towards compromise rather than victory, an echoing reminder of the mistakes of the past.

Place: United States

Time: 19th Century

ABOUT THE ART

The painter William Henry Powell was born and died in New York City at the age of 56. He was commissioned to complete a piece for the United States capitol in Washington D.C., and chose the subject of De Soto discovering the Mississippi. Hernando De Soto was a Spanish explorer from the 16th century and the first European documented to have crossed the Mississippi.

RESOLUTE

Traditional Card: Seven of Wands

Root Energy: Defense; willpower; advantage

In a Past Life:

The image on this card is of David defeating Goliath. This is a card of necessary battle. In a past life you worked through your fears to free yourself from unhealthy burdens. In this life, you are likely crossing that threshold again---challenged by something that intimidates you. This card is a reminder that there rests within you a reservoir of determination and strength, and that the universe has your back in the weeks ahead.

Alternative interpretation: At its root, this card is about conflict with an advantage. It's possible you have been put on the defensive through no fault of your own. This card reminds you to keep your cool in the situation.

Place: France

Time: 18ᵗʰ Century

ABOUT THE ART

Though the artist remains unidentified, this French painting is dated to the first half of the 18th century. It is on display in the Musée des beaux-arts de Lyon in Lyon, France.

18TH CENTURY

Traditional Card: Eight of Wands

Root Energy: Incoming action; message

In a Past Life:

The 18th Century is marked specifically by the French and American revolution. The art in this card reflects the sentiments of the French revolt. When this card appears, you spent time in this century and the freedom-lust associated with this period. It's possible you often identify chains of oppression you wish to break through in this life as well, knowing deep down you have transcended similar struggles in the past.

Alternative interpretation: This card is traditionally about an incoming message. Check email, texts and messages from loved ones for subtle meanings to uncover knowledge of a past life.

Place: Paris

Time: 18th Century

ABOUT THE ART

The painting "Freedom or Death" by Jean-Baptiste Regnault is an allegorical painting reflecting the sentiments of the French Revolution. The angelic figure is thought to be the soul of a fallen revolutionary, with both Freedom and Death embodied on either side.

Regnault was born in Paris and showed a great aptitude for art by the time he was twelve. He was promptly sent to Italy to study painting. Many of his works remain in display at the Louvre.

PRISON

Traditional Card: Nine of Wands

Root Energy: Resilience;
 imprisonment; stamina

In a Past Life:

When imprisonment has been
experienced in a past life, it can
manifest in a myriad of ways:
claustrophobia, cabin fever, and strict
adherence to the law can arise. You
are more likely to take up an active,
daily sport, and/or exercising your
freedom frequently. You are also
more likely to travel and dislike being
at home. Meditation will either be second
nature, or incredibly challenging.

Alternative interpretation: Traditionally,
this card is a message to stay strong in the
face of adversity, calling upon your
stamina and perseverance to make it
through to the other side of your struggle.
It's very possible a current, long-lasting
struggle you are experiencing relates to a
similar "imprisonment" in a previous
lifetime.

Place: Austria; Germany

Time: 19th Century

ABOUT THE ART

This 1850 painting
"Marguerite in Prison"
could represent Queen
Margaret of France, who
was imprisoned by
making enemies with her
husband, King Henry IV
of France. She was
wrongly slandered and
had a reputation for
being a nymphomaniac
as well as bearing
charges of incest with
her brother, King Henry
III.

The artist, Johann Grund
was born in Austria, and
died in Germany, having
strong ties to both
countries.

DEPRESSION

Traditional Card: Ten of Wands

Root Energy: Overburdened;
depression; overwhelmed

In a Past Life:

Depression can often be triggered by a past life experience, particularly situational depression. Although depression is biologically based, how you cope with a chemical imbalance is often rooted in your previous lifetimes. Particularly blue periods in your life now can be open wounds from a previous devastation. Losses you've suffered in this life could echo similar losses in previous lifetimes, and the pain and suffering experienced now is tenfold. Waking up on significant days of the year from a past life can bring on sudden bouts of depression and/or anxiety, seemingly out of nowhere.

Alternative interpretation: Alternatively, this card could specifically speak to the loss of an infant. If this is something you have experienced in this lifetime, know that the treasured soul you are connected to extends a message of love and comfort. Your connection is far greater than this one lifetime, and reunion is assured.

Place: Austria
Time: 18th Century

ABOUT THE ART

Peter Fendi, the creator of "Sad News" from 1838, was an Austrian court painter and a leading artist of his time. His father was a schoolmaster. He fell from a table as an infant and the injury did irreparable damage to his spine. Perhaps this trauma in his infancy played a role in selecting the subject for this painting. It's unclear whether the soldier in this painting is a threat or perhaps the father of the young children.

SON

Traditional Card: Page of Wands

Root Energy: Message; progression

In a Past Life:

This card either refers to a son you have now, or a son you had in a past life, (and sometimes these are the same person!) With the You card, this means a role reversal where you were the son, and your son/child now was your father.

.

Alternative interpretation: The page of wands is usually a messenger delivering news. In the coming weeks, expect a clear message from your guides about the journeys of your past lives and their relevance to the life you live now.

Place: United States; Germany

Time: Late 19ᵗʰ Century

ABOUT THE ART

Frank Duveneck, the artist of this 1872 painting, "The Whistling Boy" was born in Covington, Kentucky. His status as both Catholic and German made him a bit of an outsider in his community, though his artistic talent was clear. He studied painting abroad in Germany and developed a unique style that often included dark backgrounds such as the one here. His growth as an artist led him to become a household name, and Kurt Vonnegut owned one of his paintings in his private collection at one time.

TRAVELER

Traditional Card: Knight of Wands

Root Energy: Pursuit; drive

In a Past Life:

The Traveler card can be either you or someone very close to you with a good dose of wanderlust. This indicates someone who spent a significant portion of their past life on the move. Vagrant lifestyles often manifest in modern life as someone who likes to shift careers, or someone who is happiest when they are about in the world rather than reclusive at home. Artist types and free spirits often carry the energy of the traveler.

Alternative interpretation: The knight of wands is a pursuit card and often means someone pursued a person or thing with great intensity. In relationship readings, this means one person chased the other intently. If so, the experiences from a past life convinced them not to let that person get away a second time!

Place: Netherlands

Time: 17ᵗʰ Century

ABOUT THE ART

Frans van Mieris the Elder, artist of the painting "A Traveler at Rest" would become the patriarch of a family of talented portrait artists from the Netherlands. He was considered a genre painter during the Baroque period. Many of his paintings were not accurately dated and are instead relative dates.

VISIBLE WOMAN

Traditional Card: Queen of Wands

Root Energy: Artist; flirt; assertive;
 independent

In a Past Life:

The Visible Woman is a woman who gets
noticed. She's often the life of the party
and socially graceful. Christina, Queen of
Sweden, reflects classic queen of wands
energy: she defied expectations by delving
into philosophy. She often dressed as a
man in disguise and was rumored to have
a lesbian affair. She turned heads! She
rejected traditional female roles and the
Pope called her "a woman without shame."

Alternative interpretation: The queen of
wands can often appear to represent the
"other woman" in a relationship. This is
simply the other female in a love triangle,
not necessarily the one having the affair.

Place: Sweden; Netherlands

Time: 17th Century

ABOUT THE ART

Portrait artist David Beck
was born in the
Netherlands. He
eventually became part
of Christina, Queen of
Sweden's court. Near the
end of his tenure, he
asked for leave to visit
family, which she denied.
He was later found
poisoned to death.

Christina, Queen of
Sweden, is known to be
one of the most educated
queens in history. She
caused quite a stir when
she refused to marry.
Despite her strengths,
she was known to be
moody and fickle.

PHILANDERING MAN

Traditional Card: King of Wands

Root Energy: Leader; ruler; charisma

In a Past Life:

The philandering man is one who does not give his heart to one woman and is more inclined to choose his lustful desires rather than the stability of a loving partnership. King Henry VIII, famous for doing away with several wives in order to marry the next, represents the philandering man quite perfectly: fickle and self-centered, creating drama and pursuing gain in a selfish narrative that casts himself as most important. The King of Wands can often be a strong and charismatic leader, but his weakness is to think with his pants over his head and heart.

ABOUT THE ART

Lucas Horenbout, the artist of this 1540 portrait, "King Henry VIII" was born in the Flemish part of Germany. Hired by the court of England along with his father and sister, he moved to be part of Henry VIII's court. He was favored by the king and paid well. He died in England.

Alternative interpretation: The King of Wands is a strong leader and traditionally has more positive traits than negative ones, unless reversed. He is a modern-day project leader, philanthropist and showman.

Place: Germany or London

Time: 16th Century

JAPAN

Traditional Card: Ace of Swords

Root Energy: Truth; clarity;

In a Past Life:

At least a significant part of a past life was lived within Japan. You may have Japanese ancestors.

Alternative interpretation: The ace of swords usually indicates cutting through to some truth. Often, a sort of breakthrough energy accompanies this card. If Japan doesn't resonate with you, then this card may simply be saying you are about to get a moment of clarity you have been longing for.

Place: **Japan**: Established February 11, 660 BC (Aquarius/Air/Swords)

Time: 17ᵗʰ Century

ABOUT THE ART

Katsushika Taito II was born in Edo, Japan and studied under Katsushika Hokusai. It was later discovered that Taito forged Hokusai's signature on some of his paintings. It is somewhat ironic and perhaps apt that this art would appear on the card that represents the arising of truth.

GENETIC ILLNESS

Traditional Card: Two of Swords

Root Energy: Avoidance; vulnerability;
            stalemate

In a Past Life:

For this deck's purpose, the Genetic
Illness card is specifically categorized as a
cause of death. The traditional two of
swords depicts a figure blindfolded,
forming a connection to the blind figure
in this deck.

Alternative interpretation: The two of swords
is traditionally about a stalemate: a situation in
which you feel there are no good moves, so
hence you do nothing. If you are working
through an avoidance situation at this time,
there are likely past life factors influencing
both the situation itself and your emotional
response to that situation.

Place: Denmark

Time: 19ᵗʰ - Early 20ᵗʰ Century

ABOUT THE ART

Artist Anna Kirstine
Brøndum was both born
and died in Denmark. She
was the daughter of a
hotel owner, and showed
a great aptitude for art at
a young age. She studied
drawing for three years
at the Vilhelm Kyhn
College of Painting in
Copenhagen, and
eventually married
another artist, Michael
Archer. She resisted
social pressures to
devote her life to home,
and continued painting
after her marriage. Her
work was revolutionary
in how she perceived the
play of colors within
natural light. She often
painted everyday life,
subjects typically being
women and children,
such as this 1883
painting, "Blind Wife in a
Room."

BROKEN HEARTED

Traditional Card: Three of Swords

Root Energy: Heartbreak

In a Past Life:

A broken heart is usually the result of the severing of a key relationship: romance or a child are the chief causes of acute heartbreak. Death can be the cause here as well, but it usually results from words said that cannot be taken back, with one party as the aggressor and the other the victim. This heartbreak is being relived in this life, usually with the hopes of a different outcome between at least two connected souls.

Alternative interpretation: It is possible that you are having the pangs of a broken heart without any clear external reason to explain it. Ruminate on this time of year and dates. Pay close attention to dreams. Past lives will often clue us in through these channels and bring clarity to such a mental state.

Place: England

Time: 19th Century

ABOUT THE ART

Sir John Everett Millais, artist of the painting, "A Wife—Face in Both Hands She Knelt on the Carpet" was an English painter who began as a child prodigy. At eleven, he was the youngest student to ever enter the Royal Academy Schools in 1840. He eventually transitioned from Pre-Raphaelite style to his own unique perspective with realism, such as with this painting. He was a very wealthy artist in his time, but criticized by his contemporaries as a sellout for taking commissioned work for advertising.

CHRONIC ILLNESS

Traditional Card: Four of Swords

Root Energy: Rest; recovery; grief

In a Past Life:

For this deck's purpose, the Chronic Illness card is specifically categorized as a cause of death. The traditional tarot shows a figure at rest, in a healing position. This is sometimes interpreted as grief and sometimes as simply recovery (such as with a physical illness).

Alternative interpretation: For a past life reading, the four of swords would speak directly to your grief: you've lost someone whose absence is still felt, a void that cannot be filled. This card indicates a past life connection to this person, and their presence can be felt at times as they wait for you to fulfill your journey.

Place: France or England

Time: 19th Century

ABOUT THE ART

Ford Madox Brown was a French-born British painter, and the grandson of medical theorist John Brown. His daughter Emma, (aka Lucy) suffered for nearly 30 years from tuberculosis, though she led a full life including marriage and children, and a painting career of her own. She is the subject of this 1872 painting, "Convalescent."

VIOLENCE

Traditional Card: Five of Swords

Root Energy: Brutality; conquest; hostility

In a Past Life:

The violence card indicates the violence you've experienced in a past life that shapes the relationship and attitude you have with violence in this life. What others often cast as you being too sensitive in a situation is often the trauma of a past life resonating to the surface in the face of conflict.

ABOUT THE ART

Artist Jacques Stella of "The Rape of the Sabines" from 1650 was born in Lyon and died in Paris. His father, Francois Stella, was also an artist, but died too soon to train his son. Jacques spent ten years in Italy, and eventually landed a permanent position working and living in the Louvre, where he was paid well.

Alternative interpretation: Additionally, the five of swords could be suggesting that the violence you've experienced in early childhood or within a romantic relationship is situational karma in which you have hoped for a better outcome with your failed perpetrator. The disappointment from such violence is likely to impact you harder than others. This is not "deserved" violence, but instead an attempt to reconcile karma.

Place: France or Lyon

Time: 17th Century

The story of the Sabine women is that Rome's early founder, Romulus, during 8th century BC, sought women from Sabine as wives for his Roman men. The Sabines refused, so the Romans simply abducted them. Some scholars argue the word "rape" is mistranslated and that it was simply abduction.

DROWNING

Traditional Card: Six of Swords

Root Energy: Journey; leaving a bad situation into a better one; travel across water

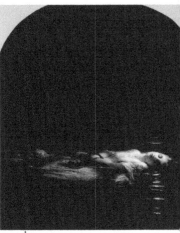

In a Past Life:

For this deck's purpose, the Drowning card is specifically categorized as a cause of death. If you drowned in a past life, you are likely to be nervous crossing bodies of water and have some deep-seated fears around swimming. Neurotic checking on a child as they bathe can simply be the trauma of the past sounding alarm bells in your mind.

Alternative interpretation: The six of swords is all about crossing stormy waters into the calm, (similar to the peace felt during the passage from life to death while drowning). This card could simply be indicating that the chaos is now in the past and a period of calm is primed to endure.

Place: France; Rome

Time: Early 19ᵗʰ Century; 4ᵗʰ Century

ABOUT THE ART

Paul Delaroche was a French painter whose subjects often involved French or English history. His style was somewhat of a mix between Romanticism and Classicism, such as this 1855 painting, "A Christian Martyr Drowned in the Tiber During the Reign of Diocletian."

Diocletian was a Roman emperor from 284-305. During the Diocletian Persecution of 303, Christians were forced to make sacrifices to pagan gods or face death. This last persecution of Christians was very bloody, but ultimately unsuccessful and Christianity would become the favored religion of Rome by 324.

BETRAYAL

Traditional Card: Seven of Swords

<u>Root Energy</u>: Betrayal; theft;
          trickery

In a Past Life:

Betrayal is at work in your
subconscious in this life based on a betrayal
you have experienced in a previous life.
Difficulty trusting without good reason is a
strong indicator that betrayal was
experienced in a past life. Paranoia or
certainty that things will go wrong can also
manifest as an indicator of past betrayals.
This card's appearance may be reflecting an
aspect of your psyche, or be specifically
addressing a betrayal you are experiencing
and/or processing now.

Alternative interpretation: This card is
traditionally the theft card and can indicate
the dishonesty of those around you, warning
that their dishonest nature will not change,
and the karma you had hoped to work out
has not progressed forward.

Place: Italy

Time: 14th Century

ABOUT THE ART

Ugolino di Nerio, the
Italian artist of this 14th
century painting, "The
Betrayal" was a leading
artist in his time. His
father and siblings were
also artists. Most of his
work contained pious
figures from Christian
narratives. He was both
born and died in Sienna.

OPPRESSION

Traditional Card: Eight of Swords

Root Energy: Isolation;
imprisonment;
restriction

In a Past Life:

Oppression can refer to literal imprisonment/slavery or it can mean oppression due to ethnicity, gender, sexuality or economic status. Oppression experienced in a past life will make you more hyper aware of these injustices as you experience them in this life. Chances are good that part of your life's path includes fighting oppression to create peace and prosperity for souls from all walks of life. Manifestations include bouts of feeling powerless and unexpected anxiety.

ABOUT THE ART

Charles William Bartlett, was born in England and died in Hawaii. He entered the Royal Academy in London when he was 23 and studied there for three years. He also spent time studying in a private studio within Paris, which is when he composed this 1888 painting, "Captives in Rome." He eventually moved to Hawaii in 1928 and spent 12 years there before his death.

Alternative interpretation: Traditionally, this card can also indicate a self-imposed restriction. This can be a firm reminder that the oppression lies in the past and that your power and capabilities to leave a situation are far greater than you feel.

Place: England and Hawaii

Time: Early 20th Century

DREAMS

Traditional Card: Nine of Swords

<u>Root Energy</u>: Anxiety; sleeplessness

In a Past Life:

The Dreams card appearing in a past life spread indicate your dreams hold valuable information to you for processing the struggles of your current life. Information in your dream state is relaying events from a past life. Although the card image is unsettling, the appearance of this card can simply be a message to pay attention to clues in your dreams.

Alternative interpretation: This card can also simply be pointing to generalized anxiety. If the dream interpretation doesn't resonate, this card is telling you that the bouts of anxiety you are currently experiencing are rooted in a past life. Often, as you pass the age that you were in a past life when a major traumatic event occurred, you will suffer a period of unexplained anxiety. This should pass in time.

<u>Place:</u> Switzerland; England

<u>Time:</u> 17th – 18th Century

ABOUT THE ART

Johann Heinrich Fussli was born in Switzerland and was the second of eighteen children. His father was also a painter. He spent much of his life in London. A large percentae of his work carries a supernatural theme, such as this 1790 painting, "The Nightmare." He also did several works based on Shakespeare and Milton. He held posts as Professor of Painting and Keeper at the Royal Academy in London.

MURDER

Traditional Card: Ten of Swords

Root Energy: A violent end; devastation; start of recovery

In a Past Life:

For this deck's purpose, the Murder card is specifically categorized as a cause of death. Because the ways in which someone can be murdered vary widely, the manifestation of the experience is difficult to deduce, as it could be psychologically reflected in a myriad of ways. Violent nightmares should provide clues to the details of this event. The appearance of this card is a healthy reminder that although your primal fears are quite valid, the threat you once experienced has been extinguished.

Alternative interpretation: Traditionally, this card is best known for its "the worst is over" message. It signifies rock bottom and reassures you that you have nowhere to go but up.

Place: France

Time: 17ᵗʰ Century

ABOUT THE ART

Trophime Bigot was a French painter who also spent 14 years (1620-1634) painting in Italy. He returned to France, where he painted this 1640 painting, "Judith Decapitating Holofernes." His style used candlelight predominantly.

The story of Judith beheading Holofernes comes from the deuterocanonical *Book of Judith*. Holofernes was an Assyrian general who was about to destroy Judith's home city of Bethulia. He desires Judith, and allows her into his tent, but he drinks too much and passes out. Judith seizes the opportunity and beheads him.

BROTHER

Traditional Card: Page of Swords

<u>Root Energy</u>: Preparation; communication; arguments

In a Past Life:

The Brother card is indicating a brother you have now with whom you share a special bond. This card could also indicate that a close male friend you have now was also once your brother.

Alternative interpretation: This is a card about planning to communicate, doing your research, and preparation. An alternative message here is that you have been planning for a particular success you are currently working on, and the work for this success stems back into the knowledge you've accumulated over lifetimes.

Place: England

Time: 18th Century

ABOUT THE ART

English painter Thomas Gainsborough was the dominant portrait artist of the second half of the 18th century. He continued on to become a founding member of the Royal Academy. He preferred painting landscape, but was often commissioned to do portraits such as this 1779 painting, "The Blue Boy." This portrait is perhaps Gainsborough's most famous painting and is said to be the portrait of Jonathan Buttall, son of a wealthy hardware merchant, though this has never been proven.

SOLDIER

Traditional Card: Knight of Swords

Root Energy: Conflict

In a Past Life:

The Soldier card indicates a past marked by war. Most likely you served as a soldier or supported a soldier in a great capacity. Look for time-period indicators to isolate which war it could have likely been.

Alternative interpretation: The knight of swords is traditionally an argumentative, fly-by-night type who acts on impulse and thinks of himself first. If that personality description matches someone around you, it could easily be indicating that soul, whether they've served in the military or not.

Place: England

Time: 19th Century

ABOUT THE ART

Octavius Oakley, artist of this 1842 watercolor portrait, "Young Officer" was an English painter who began work in a textile factory. He was eventually commissioned by the Duke of Devonshire, which began his painting career. The identity of the officer is unknown.

RATIONAL WOMAN

Traditional Card: Queen of Swords

Root Energy: Honesty; Integrity;
Academic; Rational

In a Past Life:

The Rational Woman is a highly intelligent woman who is more logical than emotional. She's likely to be articulate and more prone to think things through before acting.

Alternative interpretation: The reversed version of this card would be a cold and calculating woman with a cruel streak.

Place: England

Time: 16ᵗʰ – 17ᵗʰ Century

ABOUT THE ART

The artist of this Queen Elizabeth I painting remains unknown. Queen Elizabeth I was the child of Henry VIII and his second wife Anne Boleyn. Queen Elizabeth was known for her calculating wit, intelligence and military strategy. She was slow to act on impulse and known for sound decisions, making her an ideal Queen of Swords. Publicly, she was admired for her virginity.

RATIONAL MAN

Traditional Card: King of Swords

Root Energy: Intellect; Judgment;
           Rulership

In a Past Life:

The Rational Man is often a lawyer-type
or community leader. He is intellectual
and sharp, and more likely to be logical
than emotional.

Alternative interpretation: The reversed
version of this card would be a
manipulative man and possibly the worst
male card in the deck. However, the upright
version of the King of Swords is a good and
solid man, devoid of sentimental nonsense.

Place: Sweden; Norway

Time: 19th Century

ABOUT THE ART

Fredric Westin, Swedish
artist of this 1800s
portrait, "Karl XIV Johan,
King of Sweden and
Norway" studied at the
Royal Swedish Academy
of Arts. He was very
popular as a portrait
painter and most of his
work was of royal
families.

Karl XIV Johan, was
renowned as a brilliant
military strategist,
making him a very
suitable King of Swords.

SPAIN

Traditional Card: Ace of Pentacles

Root Energy: Inheritance; windfall

In a Past Life:

At least a significant part of a past life was lived within Spain. You may have Spanish ancestors.

ABOUT THE ART

Artist Alfred Dehodencq, painter of "A Gypsy Dance in the Gardens of the Alcazar" from 1851, was both born and died in Paris. He spent several years in Spain after an arm injury during the French Revolution of 1848. He was also one of the first painters to live within and paint scenes from Morocco.

Alternative interpretation: The ace of pentacles brings a pile of money, sometimes from an inheritance. It usually denotes the windfall of a lump sum and not necessarily the steady cash flow of employment or a safe investment.

Place: **Spain:** Established August 28, 1512 (Virgo/Earth/Pentacles)

Time: Late 19ᵗʰ Century

INDIA

Traditional Card: Two of Pentacles

<u>Root Energy</u>: Exchange; Juggling

In a Past Life:

At least a significant part of a past life was lived within India. You may have Indian ancestors.

ABOUT THE ART

Erastus Salisbury Field, artist of, "The Taj Mahal" was an American painter who showed a great aptitude for sketching by the time he was nineteen years old. He was born and lived in Massachusetts. He made a good living as a portrait painter throughout the state and the Connecticut Valley. Overall, there are over 300 surviving works from Field.

Alternative interpretation: At its basest elements, the two of pentacles is an exchange of energy: this for that. Sometimes it indicates money in, money out, such as a windfall that goes directly to meeting a debt. It sometimes appears when a sketchy partner is considering trading one romantic interest for another.

Place: **India:** India Republic established January 26, 1950 (Aquarius w/ rising Moon Taurus/Air w/ Earth/Pentacles)

Time: 19th Century

OLD AGE

Traditional Card: Three of Pentacles

Root Energy: Collaboration;
completion

In a Past Life:

When the Old Age card appears in a past
life spread, it means you were able to
complete your journey in this past life and
live into old age.

Alternative interpretation: The three of
pentacles is about working with others to
accomplish a goal, usually with tangible
results. In a past life spread, this card can be
a loving reminder that you work
collaboratively with the Divine and your
guides to fulfill your life purpose, and that
you do not have to fight alone.

Place: Netherlands

Time: 17ᵗʰ Century

ABOUT THE ART

Nicolaes Maes, (also
known as Nicolaes Maas)
was a Dutch painter who
studied in Amsterdam
under the studio of
Rembrandt. He dedicated
most of his work to the
domestic genre and
worked nearly
exclusively with
portraiture. His favorite
subjects were women
reading the bible or
cooking a meal. Many of
his female subjects were
older, such as in this
1656 painting, "An Old
Woman Praying."

GREED

Traditional Card: Four of Pentacles

Root Energy: Control; greed; miserliness

In a Past Life:

The presence of the Greed card in a spread indicates that a past life was marked by greed. You could have succumbed to a greedy nature, or you may have been the victim of another's greediness. The life you live now should provide clues to which it may be.

Alternative interpretation: The four of pentacles does not necessarily carry the negative greed connotation as presented in the card. Sometimes it simply means a temperate nature and being conservative with money. When this card appears, it indicates that the relationship and attitude you have toward money in this life is shaped by your experiences and fears from a past life.

Place: Italy

Time: 16th – 17th Century

ABOUT THE ART

Jacopo Ligozzi, the artist of this 1610 painting, "Allegory of Avarice" was an Italian painter and son of the famous painter Gvanni Ermano Ligozzi. He focused on botanical and animal subjects and was eventually invited to Florence to become one of the house artists for the Medici, an Italian banking family and political dynasty.

STARVATION

Traditional Card: Five of Pentacles

Root Energy: Loss; poverty

In a Past Life:

When the Starvation card appears, it indicates a past life marked with a period of starvation, up to and including death. If you suffered food shortage in a previous life, it is likely to influence the relationship you have with food now. A wide range of manifestations might present themselves: overeating, food avoidance, anxiety over food, or food hoarding can indicate the hauntings of starvation in a past life.

Alternative interpretation: The five of pentacles is generally about physical poverty. It includes food, but can indicate job loss, home loss and even emotional poverty after a devastating breakup or loss of a familial relationship.

Place: Germany

Time: Early 20th Century

ABOUT THE ART

Eric W. Taylor, the British artist of this 1945 sketch, "Dying from Starvation and Torture at Belsen Concentration Camp" had a long career of painting, sketching and sculpture, but is most famous for his World War II sketches and watercolor. His British troop was one of the first to enter the Bergen-Belsen Concentration Camp. At first, his depictions were of piles of bodies and general horror, but he evolved to increasingly focus on individual subjects.

CHARITY

Traditional Card: Six of Pentacles

Root Energy: Charity; karmic balance

In a Past Life:

When the Charity card appears in your spread, it most likely means you have a charitable spirit and care about the fate of the poor. This is a humanitarian quality you have developed over several lifetimes. It could also indicate that the good fortune you have enjoyed in this life is forwarded karma from your good works of charity in the past.

Alternative interpretation: The six of pentacles is a card of giving someone in need something they cannot acquire on their own. If there is someone in your life right now that needs your help, consider this a message that it is in your soul's best interest to help them.

Place: Amsterdam

Time: 16th Century

ABOUT THE ART

Pieter Aertsen, the artist of this 1575 painting, "Deeds of Christian Charity" was a Dutch painter also known as "Tall Pete" due to his height. He is credited with creating the monumental genre scene, a combination of still life and genre painting, with great detail and realistic features given to everyday items. Unlike some of his contemporaries, his female figures were less comedic and more dignified.

17ᵀᴴ CENTURY

Traditional Card: Seven of Pentacles

<u>Root Energy</u>: Investment

In a Past Life:

The 17ᵗʰ Century was marked by exploration of the American and Australian continents, several key writings by Shakespeare, and the work of Galileo.

Alternative interpretation: The seven of pentacles is traditionally a card of harvest, planting seeds and waiting for the plants to sprout and the crop to litter the fields. This card can sometimes indicate a period of waiting. Conversely, it can indicate the gains from an investment are forthcoming, after an adequate period of time.

Place: Netherlands

Time: 17ᵗʰ Century

ABOUT THE ART

The Dutch School were painters from the Netherlands from the Early Renaissance to the Baroque period. Art labeled "Dutch School" simply means the individual artist couldn't be identified. There was an abundance of art production in Denmark during the 17th Century. This painting, "Joust on the Hofvijver" perhaps depicts a sense of what that era was like.

GREECE

Traditional Card: Eight of Pentacles

<u>Root Energy</u>: Apprenticeship

In a Past Life:

At least a significant part of a past life was lived within Greece. You may have Greek ancestors. Ancient Greece is also notorious for the city of Lesbos, an island known for the lesbian lifestyle. This card could also indicate a lesbian or homosexual partnership.

Alternative interpretation: The eight of pentacles typically indicates a course of study or apprenticeship through which a person learns a new skill, trade, or career. This card could possibly be indicating that the course of study you are now on is shaped in some way by past life events and desires.

Place: Greece

Time: 19th Century

ABOUT THE ART

Simeon Solomon was one of eight children, three of whom showed a great aptitude for art. Simeon learned painting from his older brother Abraham, and his sister Rebecca exhibited art at the Royal Academy in 1852, where Simeon would also study and thrive. His career was cut short in 1873 when he was arrested at a public urinal on Oxford Street for attempting sodomy, and had to pay a fine. He was arrested again in 1874 in Paris for similar charges, and had to serve three months in prison. His art became popular among other gay artists at the time such as Oscar Wilde. He was known for homosexual themes, such as this 1864 painting, "Sappho and Erinna in a Garden at Myllene."

19ᵀᴴ CENTURY

Traditional Card: Nine of Pentacles

Root Energy: Financial independence

In a Past Life:

The 19ᵗʰ Century was an exciting period of enhanced transportation and industrialization. This period saw a significant amount of prosperity and stability, particularly in contrast to previous centuries.

Alternative interpretation: The nine of pentacles is the card of financial independence and stability. This card could be indicating a past life of personal success and self-reliance. An innate confidence often manifests if the nine of pentacles is part of a past life.

Place: Hungary

Time: 19ᵗʰ Century

ABOUT THE ART

Jozsef Boros, the Hungarian artist of this 1852 painting, "The Dissatisfied Painter" had a prolific career as an artist up until 1861. He lost a considerable amount of money in the stock market, and opened a photography business since painting was failing to keep up with the photography market at the time. He died as a restaurant owner in 1883.

MEXICO

Traditional Card: Ten of Pentacles

Root Energy: Family; contentment

In a Past Life:

At least a significant part of a past life was lived within Mexico. You may have native or Spanish ancestors.

ABOUT THE ART

Carl Nebel was a German architect and engineer best known for his Mexican paintings during the Mexican-American War from 1846-48. After his studies in art in Hamburg and Paris, he moved to Mexico and became a resident of the country from 1829-1834. He sold his collections in Paris, including this 1836 painting, "Las Tortilleras."

Alternative interpretation: The ten of pentacles is the card of a happy home life. Not only do you have a happy family surrounding and supporting you, you also have plenty of resources to live comfortably. For a past life spread, this card indicates a life of contentment is within reach and that you have been building to this accomplishment over several lifetimes.

Place: **Mexico:** Established September 16, 1810 (Virgo/Earth/Pentacles)

Time: 19th Century

SISTER

Traditional Card: Page of Pentacles

Root Energy: Project; achievement

In a Past Life:

The Sister card is indicating a sister you have now with whom you share a special bond. This card could also indicate that a close female friend you have now was also once your sister.

Alternative interpretation: The page of pentacles usually represents a project that can bring groundbreaking success. Whatever this goal may be, its development and manifestation have been building over several lifetimes.

Place: Unclear

Time: Early 19ᵗʰ Century

ABOUT THE ART

This painting, "Portrait of a Young Swiss Girl" comes from Switzerland around 1800. Very little of the painting is known, though her race is noteworthy and raises probing questions about her narrative. This was at one time thought to be the work of Swiss painter Jean Etienne Liotard.

TRUE FRIEND

Traditional Card: Knight of Pentacles

<u>Root Energy</u>: Arrival; steadfast;
          dependability

In a Past Life:

The true friend points to a good and
trustworthy friend you have in this life and
who has supported you as a true friend in
a past life as well. There exists between
you a natural and trusting bond, one that
others often observe and envy. This friend
will not let you down or abandon you
when times are difficult.

Alternative interpretation: The knight of
pentacles carries the energy of something or
someone arriving and staying for the long
haul. This card can simply indicate the
endurance of a relationship sustained through
multiple lives, whether this relationship is a
friendship or not. This card can also appear
right before you meet a significant person
with whom you share a past life connection.

Place: Netherlands

Time: 16th Century

ABOUT THE ART

Dutch painter Jan
Mostaert claimed to be
descended from the
Haarlem knights of the
Crusade to Damietta. He
was hired by Margaret of
Austria for his
portraiture. It is believed
that the African man in
this 16th century portrait
was either part of
Margaret's court, or
perhaps the bodyguard
of Charles V, who had a
black archer, Christophle
le More. The man's
clothing, sword and
gloves are all indicators
of his wealth and status
and suggest Portuguese
or Spanish origins. Many
of the Africans who came
to Europe during this
time were advisors and
scholars.

INDIGENOUS WOMAN

Traditional Card: Queen of Pentacles

Root Energy: Mother; pregnancy;
dependable woman

In a Past Life:

The indigenous woman could simply
be indicating an ethnicity: one that's
rooted to traditionally earth-centric
cultures. The Queen of Pentacles is
recognizable by her consistent and
dependable nature: a woman who is
the rock of her home, and whom you
can depend on to be there for you
whenever life lets you down.

Alternative interpretation: The queen of
pentacles can sometimes indicate pregnancy.
In a past life reading, this would be the
announcement of a new incarnation from a
past life connection. She can often represent
the mother.

Place: American Continent

Time: Early 20th Century

ABOUT THE ART

The woman in this 1830
portrait is believed to be
Pe-o-ka, wife of the
Seminole chief, Osceola,
and their son, though the
artist remains unknown.
Osceola was of mixed
race, Creek Indian and
English, which accounts
for the European
features of the child.

INDIGENOUS MAN

Traditional Card: King of Pentacles

<u>Root Energy</u>: Wealth;
　　　　　　dependable man

In a Past Life:

The indigenous man could be indicating the ethnicity of a past life, one rooted to traditionally earth-centric cultures. The King of Pentacles is recognized by his inclination to save money rather than spend, his wealth, his generous nature, and his willingness to settle down in a relationship.

Alternative interpretation: The king of pentacles can simply herald wealth and stability it general. If you have a frugal yet generous nature, this might simply be reflected in this card rather than representing a person. Your inner balance of temperance and goodwill is a strong quality you have developed over many lives.

Place: United States

Time: 19th Century

ABOUT THE ART

American George Catlin, artist of this 1832 portrait, "Buffalo Bull's Back Fat" was known for his American Indian art from the Old West. Catlin took five trips west from 1830-1836 and always held a strong passion and fascination for American Indians.

Buffalo Bull's Back Fat (the most delicious part of the buffalo) was a chief of the Blood Indians and according to Catlin, was about 50 years old at the time of the sitting. His own warriors as well as natives from enemy tribes, such as Crow and Cree, surrounded the chief and artist during the sitting.

Would you like a reading with Melanny? Send a message to the Red Orchid Publishing Facebook page, or send private email inquiries to:

redorchidpublishing@gmail.com

Don't forget to check out this deck's accompanying coursework, *The Past Lives Workbook: 21 Days to Understanding Yourself,* and other great products at:

www.redorchidpublishing.com

Made in the USA
Las Vegas, NV
06 June 2024

90778734R00049